D1519087

FROM Cone TO Pine Tree

EMMA CARLSON BERNE

LERNER PUBLICATIONS Minneapolis

Lerner Publications Company
A division of Lerner Publishing Group, Inc.
241 First Avenue North
Minneapolis, MN 55401 USA

For reading levels and more information, look up this title at www.lernerbooks.com.

Library of Congress Cataloging-in-Publication Data

Names: Berne, Emma Carlson, author.
Title: From cone to pine tree / Emma Carlson Berne.
Other titles: Start to finish (Minneapolis, Minn.). Second series.
Description: Minneapolis : Lerner Publications, 2017. | Series: Start to finish. Second series | Includes bibliographical references and index.
Identifiers: LCCN 2016037278 (print) | LCCN 2016038338 (ebook) | ISBN 9781512434446 (lb) | ISBN 9781512450965 (eb pdf)
Subjects: LCSH: Pine—Life cycles—Juvenile literature.
Classification: LCC QK494.5.P66 B47 2017 (print) | LCC QK494.5.P66 (ebook) | DDC 585/.2—dc23

LC record available at https://lccn.loc.gov/2016037278

Manufactured in the United States of America
1-42093-25387-10/20/2016

TABLE OF Contents

Pinecones grow into trees. How do they do it?

A pine tree makes pinecones.

Pine trees make male pinecones and female pinecones.
Male pinecones grow near the bottom of the tree.
Female pinecones grow farther up.

The pinecones make pollen and egg cells.

Male pinecones make pollen, and female pinecones make egg cells. The pollen and the egg cells need to come together for more trees to be made.

The pinecones let their pollen out.

When the air **temperature** is just right in the spring, the male pinecones open up. They let their pollen out. It falls to the ground.

The pollen fertilizes the egg cells.

Wind carries the pollen up near the top of the pine tree, where the female pinecones grow. The pollen lands on the female cones. It **combines** with the egg cells inside the female cones. This is called fertilization.

11

Next, seeds grow inside the pinecones.

After fertilization, seeds begin to grow inside the female pinecones. But fertilization takes a long time. It can take a whole year! In that year, the female pinecones grow too. They turn into the large, woody cones you may have seen.

The cones protect the pine tree seeds.

As the seeds and female cones grow, the cones shelter the seeds. The hard wood outside the cones keeps the seeds safe inside. Even **mature** seeds stay safe. They are tucked between the petals of the cone.

Then the pinecones open up.

Once all the seeds are mature, the pinecones are ready to scatter the seeds. The cones open up their petals. Now the seeds can get out!

The pinecones scatter their seeds.

The pinecones release the seeds into the air. Wind and animals help scatter the seeds so they can land in good spots to grow.

The seeds grow into pine trees.

Seeds that land in good soil push down roots and push up needles. They grow into baby pine trees. Little trees get bigger. When the trees are grown, they make male and female pinecones. The cycle begins again!

Glossary

combines: blends together

egg cells: very small parts that form an egg

fertilizes: mixes with egg cells to make new life

mature: fully grown

pollen: a powder that a male plant releases

temperature: how hot or cold something is

Further Information

Doudna, Kelly. *Super Simple Pinecone Projects: Fun and Easy Crafts Inspired by Nature.* Minneapolis: Abdo, 2014. Use your hands and your brain to make interesting crafts and art with pinecones.

Kids.gov: Plants
https://kids.usa.gov/science/plants/index.shtml
Visit this US government site just for kids to learn all about gardening, nature, and plants.

National Wildlife Federation Kids: Go on a Conifer Quest
http://www.nwf.org/kids/family-fun/outdoor-activities/conifer-quest.aspx
Try this fun activity with an adult to learn more about trees.

Pipe, Jim. *You Wouldn't Want to Live without Trees!* New York: Franklin Watts, 2017. Learn everything you've ever wanted to know about trees in this general fact guide.

Russo, Monica. *Treecology: 30 Activities and Observations for Exploring the World of Trees and Forests.* Chicago: Chicago Review, 2016. Take your knowledge outdoors with this activity book about nature.

Index

Photo Acknowledgments
The images in this book are used with the permission of: © iStockphoto.com/Smileus, p. 1; © iStockphoto.com/DNY59, p. 3; © Thomas Smith/Alamy, p. 5; © Manuela Schewe-Behnisch/EyeEm/Getty Images, p. 7; © Jim Reed/Corbis Documentary/Getty Images, p. 9; © Art Directors & TRIP/Alamy, p. 11; © Arco Images GmbH/Alamy, p. 13; © WildPictures/Alamy, p. 15; © omphoto/Bigstock.com, p. 17; © Design Pics Inc/Alamy, p. 19; © imageBROKER/Alamy, p. 21.

Front cover: © Seagull J/Bigstock.com.

Main body text set in Arta Std Book 20/26.
Typeface provided by International Typeface Corp.

LERNER
SOURCE™

Expand learning beyond the printed book. Download free, complementary educational resources for this book from our website, www.lerneresource.com.